FLIGHT SQUADS

BY EMILY SCHLESINGER

NONFICTION

Cryptocurrency

Deadly Bites

Droids and Robots

Flight Squads

www.sdlback.com

Photo credits: page 9: stocknadia / Shutterstock.com; page 12: jiawangkun / Shutterstock.com; page 13: Olga Steckel / Shutterstock.com; page 17: BlueBarronPhoto / Shutterstock.com; pages 18-19: Comaniciu Dan / Shutterstock.com; page 22: Chris Parypa Photography / Shutterstock.com; page 23: Mike V. Shuman / Shutterstock.com; page 25: Chris Parypa Photography / Shutterstock.com; pages 26-27: Brian Dote / Shutterstock.com; page 29: Olga Steckel / Shutterstock.com; page 32: Tetra Images / Alamy Stock Photo; page 37: PJF Military Collection / Alamy Stock Photo; page 39: AB Forces News / Alamy Stock Photo; page 41: AB Forces News Collection / Alamy Stock Photo; page 47: Chris Parypa Photography / Shutterstock.com; pages 48-49: Barney Low / Alamy Stock Photo; page 51: PJF Military Collection / Alamy Stock Photo; page 53: Scott J Ferrel/Congressional Quarterly / Alamy Stock Photo; page 57: Xinhua / Alamy Stock Photo; All other source images from Shutterstock.com

ISBN-13: 978-1-68021-691-2
eBook: 978-1-63078-478-2

Printed in Malaysia

23 22 21 20 19   1 2 3 4 5

Table of Contents

1 Formation

The commander speaks first. "Diamond burner go. Right turn off."

Pilots chime in.

"Sure," says #2.

"Let's go," says #4.

The commander speaks again. "Left turn. Diamond dirty clean flat pass."

"Perfect," says #3.

The commander continues. "Now roll it. Break out. Join at the top of the loop. Here comes a G. Get after it!" Pilots brace.

"Coming left. Smoke on. Pull. Smoke off. Push. Take it in. Easing power. Easy brakes. Shut down."

"Emergency brakes," says #3.

"Brakes released," say all.

The planes are on the ground. Everyone has landed safely. All breathe quiet sighs of relief.

Back at the Office

It is the next morning before dawn. The pilots sit around a conference table. Their eyes blink in the fluorescent light. Each pilot clutches a pen. They hold it like the control stick of a jet. The location is a small building. It is deep in the Sonoran Desert. This is a pre-dawn briefing. The team talks through the day's flight.

Once in air, planes fly up to 700 miles per hour. They travel in a tight formation. There are rapid force changes. Some moves are upside-down. Pilots push the limits of what jets can do. In order to do this, minds must be ready. The team prepares for the flight. There can be no mistakes. Those are deadly. The team is a flight demonstration squadron. These pilots represent the best of the U.S. military.

FAST FACT: Members of flight squads are not paid differently than the rest of the military. Their salaries are based on rank and years of service.

2 Flight Demonstration Squads

The U.S. military has two flight demonstration squads. One is the Blue Angels. This team is part of the **Navy**. **Marines** are included too. The other team is the Thunderbirds. They fly for the **Air Force**. Both teams feature top fighter pilots. Planes are lightning fast.

The teams perform around the country. There are over 100 shows a year. Up to one million people go to watch. Why? Six planes fly at once while doing daring moves. This is called **aerobatics**. It is what makes the shows famous.

FAST FACT: The first flight squad was formed in 1931 in France. They are called the Patrouille de France.

The Mission

The teams fly fighter planes, but they do not fight.
No guns or bombs are onboard. Their mission is
different. The goal is to engage the public. The pilots
share their military expertise with Americans across
the country. Skills are on display. Courage and
teamwork are too. For these pilots, character is as
important as flying skill.

The teams represent nearly a million service
members. Each pilot gives their all. Nothing less
than their best is good enough. This is the culture of
the military.

Both teams display their pride. The shows make the public proud too. This helps recruit new service members. Young people are inspired. They join a branch of the military. The next generation takes shape.

FLIGHT STATS

The Blue Angels' home is the Naval Air Station in Pensacola, Florida. The Thunderbirds are based at Nellis Air Force Base in Nevada. Both teams perform at air shows in dozens of states each year. They also appear at special events, such as Super Bowl games.

3 Blue Angels

The Blue Angels fly like something out of the future. But their story began in 1946. It was the end of World War II. Admiral Nimitz was the top Navy officer. Navy planes had helped defeat Japan.

When the war ended, Nimitz had a concern. Americans might forget the Navy. It worried him because the Navy still needed their support. He had an idea for an air show. His goal was to keep the public interested. People would see the Navy's flying skill.

Butch Voris led the team. He was a top fighter pilot. The team flew Hellcat planes. That was a type of plane that helped win the war.

The first show was in Jacksonville, Florida. Planes flew at amazing speeds. The way they moved shocked the audience. People were spellbound. More shows followed.

The team still did not have a name. A magazine changed that. One pilot was reading *The New Yorker*. He saw the name of a nightclub. It was called *The Blue Angel*. He loved the name. Everyone else on the team did too. That settled it. Their name became the Blue Angels.

The team's moves would become legendary. One was the diamond. Four planes zoomed in a tight pack. They formed a diamond shape. Wings nearly touched. Another move was the loop. Planes flew upside down in a circle. There was the barrel roll too. Planes spun as they flew.

FAST FACT: Many of the flying techniques used by the Blue Angels are the same as they were in 1946.

The Korean War

In 1950, the fun ended. The U.S. went to war again. This was the Korean War. All pilots were needed. The Blue Angels volunteered to fight. The team shot rockets over Korea. John Magda was one of the pilots. Gunfire struck his plane. Magna did not survive. He was honored after his death. An award was given for brave combat. This is called the Navy Cross.

The Navy made a decision. The Blue Angels would not fight again. They would keep their original mission. This was flight demonstration. Their job was to inspire the public.

The Hornet

The shows grew over the years. More people attended. New moves were added. Planes became faster. The Hellcat was replaced by the Bearcat. Next was the Panther. Then came the Cougar and the Tiger. The Phantom and Skyhawk followed. In 1986, the Blue Angels turned 40. They unveiled the F-18 Hornet. This model is still used today.

AIRCRAFT MODIFICATIONS

The F-18 Hornet is a fighter plane. Many changes must be made to convert it to a demonstration plane. Weapons are removed. Some equipment is added. An inverted fuel tank allows planes to fly upside-down. A smoke-oil tank creates a smoke trail. This shows the plane's path through the sky. Finally, a spring is added to the control stick. The extra 40 pounds of tension makes it harder to push. This allows for more precise control.

The Hornet

MODEL NAME: BOEING F/A-18 HORNET

PRICE: $21 MILLION

TOP SPEED: 1,400 MPH

USED BY BLUE ANGELS:
NOVEMBER 1986-PRESENT

WEIGHT: 24,500 POUNDS

LENGTH: 56 FEET

WINGSPAN: 40 FEET, 5 INCHES

HEIGHT: 15 FEET, 4 INCHES

4 Thunderbirds

Another story began after World War II. It was 1947. The Air Force had grown. It became its own branch of the military. Then the Korean war hit. Air Force jets did much of the fighting. These were F-84s. They were also called Thunderstreaks. The U.S. government wanted to show what the jets could do. It ordered the Air Force to set up a flight demonstration team. This happened in 1953.

The team needed a name. An answer was found nearby. Native Americans lived in the area. They had a legend. It was about a bird with superpowers. Some said it was an eagle. Others said it was a hawk. It was called *thunderbird*. A decision did not take long. Thunderbirds became the team's name.

Breaking Barriers

Early Thunderbird shows lasted 15 minutes.
The team did aerobatics. There were also solo
performances. This is when one plane does stunts
alone.

The team showed off the latest planes. In 1956, they
made history with the Super Sabre. It got its name
for being supersonic. This means it flew faster than
Mach 1. That is faster than the speed of sound. In
1969, a plane flew even faster. The F-4 Phantom
could reach Mach 2. That is twice the speed of
sound.

Fast speeds cause friction. This is a force between a plane and the air. It generates heat. Planes needed protection. They got a special paint job. A white paint resisted heat. The Thunderbirds' planes were painted this way. Red and blue paint were added too. Their famous look was created.

SONIC BOOM

Sound travels in waves. If a plane flies fast enough, it pushes against its own sound waves. These start to build up in front of the plane. They form a high-pressure area. When the plane breaks through this area, the pressure is suddenly released. This creates a sonic boom heard from the ground. It sounds like a thunder clap.

In 1982, a new model arrived. It was the F-16 Fighting Falcon. The team flies Fighting Falcons up to this day.

The Thunderbirds and Blue Angels have similar goals. This has led to competition. Sometimes the teams performed near each other. People compared them. Who put on a better show? The military decided this was not a good thing. The purpose was not to compete. A new rule was created. Teams would not fly within 150 miles of each other.

FAST FACT: In addition to their responsibilities as part of the flight demonstration team, the Thunderbirds are part of our combat force. If needed, the aircraft can be made ready for combat in less than 72 hours.

Fighting Falcon

WEIGHT: 19,700 POUNDS

PRICE: $18.8 MILLION

TOP SPEED: 1,500 MPH

MODEL NAME: LOCKHEED MARTIN F-16C FIGHTING FALCON

USED BY THUNDERBIRDS:
1982 TO 1991 (F-16A)
1992 TO PRESENT (F-16C)

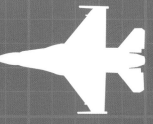

LENGTH: 49 FEET, 5 INCHES

WINGSPAN:
32 FEET, 8 INCHES

HEIGHT: 16 FEET

CHAPTER 5

Showtime

It is showtime. Crowds gather in an open area. Each event is free. Hot dogs and ice cream are sold at food stands. Fans put on hats and slather on sunscreen. They will be staring at the sky for a long time.

A show may include 30 maneuvers. Only 15 seconds separate each one. Teams don't want the audience to get bored.

Diamond Formation

The basic formation is the diamond. Many maneuvers are based on it. One is the Diamond Loop. Four planes form a diamond. Then they make an upside-down loop. The distance between them never changes. It is as if the planes are one.

The Diamond Vertical Break is another. Four planes are positioned in a diamond shape. They fly straight up. At 6,000 feet, the diamond breaks. Each plane flies a different way. Their jet trails look like the leaves of a palm tree.

FLIGHT TEAMS

Both teams assign a number to each pilot. Pilots #1–4 mostly fly in formations such as the diamond. Pilots #5 and #6 demonstrate solo moves. Sometimes all six pilots fly together.

#1 Commander: leader in charge of the entire squadron; flies at the front of the diamond

#2 Left Wing: flies to the left in the diamond

#3 Right Wing: flies to the right in the diamond

#4 Slot Pilot: flies at the rear of the diamond

#5 Lead Solo: shows off high-performance capabilities

#6 Opposing Solo: joins the lead solo for stunts

Delta Formation

Six planes form a triangle. This is called a delta. In the Delta Roll, the whole triangle spins. Planes tilt sideways as they fly. The triangle never breaks. It makes a corkscrew in the sky.

Then there is the Delta Burst. Six planes fly toward the crowd. When the planes get close, they each break away. The planes fly in six different directions.

Opposing Solos

There are moves that use two solo planes. Pilots often mirror a move. One example is the Opposing Knife Edge. Two planes fly straight toward each other. It looks like they will crash. Just before the planes meet, each plane flips. Now the planes are sideways. Planes pass belly-to-belly.

Another move makes fans gape. One plane flies normally. Above it is a second plane. That one is upside-down. Their tails look as though they touch.

Planes are as little as 18 inches apart. How do they fly so close? Some people think computers do it, but that is not the case. It is human effort. Pilots steer with precision. This takes extreme focus.

FAST FACT: Until 1956, planes in air shows could fly at supersonic speeds, which is faster than the speed of sound. Then the Federal Aviation Administration made a rule. Planes could not go that fast during demonstrations. Today, the highest speed flown at an air show is 700 miles per hour. The lowest speed is 120 miles per hour.

CHAPTER

6 # G-Force

Imagine you're on a roller coaster. Cars
climb the track. They pick up speed. Your
body presses against the seat. A wide grin
stretches across your face. Suddenly the
car stops. You jerk forward.

A force had pulled you back. Then it pushed you forward. It is called **G-force**. This is felt when you change speed. G-forces are felt in all planes, but they are felt most in fighter jets. These **accelerate** fast. They do quick moves. Pilots are pushed back in their seats.

G-force is measured in "Gs." A Hornet can pull 8 Gs. This means 8 times the force of gravity. An F-16 can reach 9 Gs. G-force makes the body feel heavier. 9 Gs feels like 9 times body weight. Pilots might feel like they weigh 1,500 pounds.

FAST FACT: A ride called Tower of Terror has the record for the highest G-force on a roller coaster. It is 6.3 Gs. The coaster is located at a theme park in South Africa.

G-Force and the Body

G-force is not just a feeling. It has dangerous effects. Blood rushes from the brain. It flows down to legs and feet. Even a small loss makes people dizzy. Worse, it may cause fainting. A large G-force can make pilots pass out. They could lose control of a plane.

A G-suit helps. Many fighter pilots and astronauts wear one. How does it work? The suit has air inside. It squeezes the legs and stomach. Blood does not leave the brain. Thunderbirds wear G-suits, but Blue Angels don't. Why? It is because of their planes. Air makes G-suits expand. They push against the controls. This affects steering.

Blue Angel pilots have another way to fight Gs. They do it with their muscles. Pilots accelerate. G-forces rise. Pilots clench their stomach and legs. Muscles tense hard. Blood stays in the brain. Pilots must do this every time. Otherwise they will pass out. Their planes could crash.

Sometimes G-force is extreme. Then pilots do the "full hick maneuver." They make a loud grunt. It sounds like "Hick!" Part of the throat closes. This cuts off flow from the brain. The Thunderbirds use these exercises too. G-suits only help so much. Muscles must do the rest.

TOO MUCH G-FORCE?

A-LOC stands for Almost Loss of Consciousness. It is the condition caused by G-force. A pilot nearly passed out, becoming confused and drowsy. G-LOC is when pilots black out entirely. A-LOC and G-LOC are one of the top causes of accidents for flight demonstration pilots.

Flight Prep

Bodies must be strong to fight Gs. That is why pilots work out. They pump iron almost every day. It is like being a pro athlete. "We hit the gym hard," says Mark Tedrow. "We work on our core muscle groups." Tedrow was Blue Angel #5.

Diet keeps energy high. Most meals include meat. This helps build muscle. Vegetables keep pilots in top form. Pilots avoid simple carbs. Sugar and white flour cause drowsiness. Pilots drink water throughout the day. Muscles stay **hydrated**. Reflexes are fast.

Making the Team

Pilots must be fit. What else does it take to be on the team? The application process is long. Only military pilots can apply. They must have flown at least 1,000 hours. This includes challenging missions. Pilots also must have served in combat.

Character is important too. Pilots must be hardworking. They must be team players. Communicating well is a must. What else? "It takes heart," says one Thunderbird. Pilots must have the right spirit. It is hard to define, but the team knows it when they see it.

Training

Show season is March to November. Training is in winter. It lasts ten weeks. The schedule is intense. Pilots fly three times a day. They do this six days a week.

"That is a grind," says Russ Bartlett. Bartlett was a Thunderbird commander. Training was part of his job. He told new pilots the truth. The experience would be a "gut check." Nothing in his life had been harder. But it was also "absolutely awesome."

TRAINING ZONE

The Blue Angels have trained in El Centro, California, for over 50 years. This is nearly 1,700 miles from their base in Pensacola, Florida. Why would they practice so far from home? El Centro has perfect winter flying conditions. The Blue Angels practice in a large section of the desert known as Restricted Area 2510, or "Shade Tree Bomb Range." It is almost always sunny there. The land is almost completely flat.

Dangers

Blue Angels seem to defy gravity. Thunderbirds travel at speeds that stun. Yet many pilots call the job safe. How can this be?

Safety is a top goal. Long checklists are followed. Rules are memorized. Crews check planes before every flight.

Are radios 1 and 2 working?

Check.

Is smoke pressure on?

Check.

The list goes on and on. It takes time to get through it. Nothing is ever skipped.

The next step is a weather forecast. Wind speed is checked. Temperature and air pressure are checked too. Skies must be safe for flying.

THE CREW BEHIND THE TEAM

Pilots are the celebrities at air shows. But they are only a small part of the team. Each squadron has over a hundred crew members. These people do most of the work. This includes all maintenance. They are responsible for the safety of the planes. The Blue Angels say their crew "owns the planes." Every show takes 14 hours of maintenance work. Traveling each week is a huge task as well. The crew loads 60,000 pounds of cargo in less than 20 minutes. This includes plane parts, radios, computers, and luggage.

Pilots also check in with themselves. Did they sleep well? Are they alert? Do they feel ill? If anything is wrong, pilots do not go up.

Something may go wrong. A plane is about to crash. The pilot needs to get out fast. Every plane has an ejection seat. It works by pulling a handle. This **ejects** the pilot from the plane. Then a parachute opens, and the seat falls away. The pilot is carried to safety.

If rules are followed, flying is mostly safe. But mistakes happen.

Double Crash

On June 2, 2016, two planes crashed on the same day. One was a Thunderbird plane. The other was a Blue Angel.

The Thunderbirds were giving a show. It was in Colorado. A plane went down. The pilot ejected. No one was hurt.

The other crash was deadly. It happened in Tennessee. A Blue Angel did a "Split S" move. But he started too low. He was also going too fast. There was no time to eject. The plane hit the ground.

G-Force Errors

Another crash happened in 2007. This was in South Carolina. G-force reached 6 Gs. The pilot did not react. He became confused. Then he lost control of the plane. Eight people on the ground were hurt.

In 1999, two pilots lost their lives. This was in Georgia. Their plane went down. The cause is unknown. But one pilot had a hurt rib. This may have made it hard to tense muscles. G-forces could have made him pass out.

WALL OF FIRE

The Diamond Crash

The worst crash may have been in 1982. The Thunderbirds were in the Nevada desert. Four planes dove into a loop. But they were too low. The first plane hit the ground. Then the rest followed. All four pilots were killed.

When an accident happens, there is an investigation. The military learns from the mistake. Rules are changed. Safety steps are improved. Flying always has risks. But the goal is to make it safe.

FAST FACT: Flight squads have a maneuver known as the Wall of Fire. This move uses a combination of bombs and gasoline.

Community Inspiration

Each team has a mission. The aims
are similar. Honor service members.
Demonstrate the best of the military. This
is done mainly through air shows. Flying
plays a big part. But the mission does
not end there. Community also plays a
role. The Blue Angels call it "community
outreach." The Thunderbirds use the term
"people-to-people programs."

Tom Frosch commanded the Blue Angels for three years. He calls them a face for the Navy. Frosch and his team did over 5,000 hours of community service. They built housing and worked at food banks. Team members visited schools and hospitals.

The Thunderbirds also give back to the community. They call themselves "America's Ambassadors in Blue."

All service members make **sacrifices**. The teams honor this spirit. They give their time and strength to help others.

Inspiring Excellence

Being a Blue Angel is a great honor. For some, talking with the community is the best part. Katie Higgins thinks so. She served for two years. "I loved the idea of going out and inspiring excellence," she says. Higgins was the first woman Blue Angel pilot. She inspired a Twitter hashtag. It is #flieslikeagirl.

Higgins met many children at shows. Their beliefs surprised her. Many did not know women could be pilots. Others did not know women could be in the military. Higgins set the record straight. She encouraged both girls and boys to go after their dreams. Her hope is that she made a difference in their lives.

THE FIRST WOMAN

When Nicole Malachowski was in 6th grade, her teacher asked what she wanted to be when she grew up. Nicole answered, "A fighter pilot." Her teacher suggested she choose something else. There were no female fighter pilots. Nicole refused. In 2005, she made history. She became the first woman flight demonstration pilot in the U.S. military. She was Thunderbird #3.

FAST FACT: Women were not allowed to fly U.S. military combat aircraft until 1993.

Passing It On

The Thunderbirds changed Lloyd Newton's life.
Newton saw the Thunderbirds in 1964. He decided
he would be one. Ten years later, he made the team.
Newton was the first black Thunderbird pilot. Later,
he became a four-star general.

Flying inspired Newton. His dream was to pass this
inspiration on. To do that, he became Commander of
Air Education. Newton inspired new generations of
pilots. In one program, young people train in flying.
They get college credit for these hours. This turns
flying into a degree.

The country needs more people in science and math fields. Newton believes flying is a perfect recruiting tool. Kids get interested in flying. It lights a fire. Many go on to careers in math and science.

Newton visits schools around the country. He tells students the same things. Sit down. List your goals. Write your dreams. Then go for them. Opportunities are out there. They are greater than most of us expect.

10 Riding High

What is it like being a Blue Angel or a Thunderbird? Nick Eberling called it "a ride like no other." He was Thunderbird #5. Eberling thinks it is the best job in the world. People have a need for speed, explains Eberling. He got a thrill from riding an F-16. It put out 30,000 pounds of **thrust**. That is like being shot out of a cannon.

Jason Heard agrees. He served as Thunderbird #1. "It's loud, it's fast, it's fun," he says. He also admires the culture of teamwork. No one does anything alone, Heard explains. Each team member puts the needs of others first.

Ryan Chamberlain was a Blue Angel. He was lead solo. What was the best part for him? It was telling the story of the Navy and Marines. "I will probably miss that the most," he said.

Steve Horton may sum it up best. He was a Thunderbird slot pilot. Horton would hear people talking after shows. Many said they were proud to be Americans. They were proud of the military. People had tears in their eyes. Horton says, "That's just the best feeling of all."

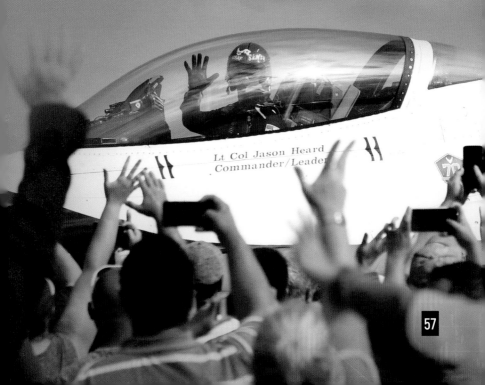

Lt Col Jason Heard
Commander/Leader

Glossary

accelerate: to speed up

aerobatics: impressive moves done by planes in the air

Air Force: a branch of the U.S. military that operates from the air

combat: fighting between military groups

eject: to suddenly be pushed out

formation: when a group of planes flies in a certain shape

friction: force caused by one object rubbing against another

G-force: a force that pushes an object backward or forward when speed changes

G-suit: a suit that squeezes the body to prevent blood from leaving the head during flying

hydrated: having enough water

maneuver: a planned movement done by an aircraft

Marines: a branch of the U.S. military that operates both on land and at sea

Navy: a branch of the U.S. military that works at sea

precision: being exact and accurate

recruit: to get new people to join an organization

sacrifice: giving up something for the sake of helping someone else

solo: performed alone

squadron: a flying team made up of pilots, crew, and planes

supersonic: able to travel faster than the speed of sound

thrust: the force of an engine pushing a jet forward

TAKE A LOOK INSIDE
DEADLY BITES

Forest and Ice

Some think bears are cute. They look like stuffed animals. Because of that, some think they must be harmless. This is not accurate. Bears kill.

Grizzly Bears

Grizzlies are a kind of brown bear. They used to fear people. That changed over 50 years ago. National Parks had open garbage pits. Campers kept food near tents. Bears started to **scavenge** for food. They got close to people. Bears stopped being scared.

One attacked on August 13, 1967. This was at Glacier National Park. The bear killed a woman. An attack had not happened in the park's history of more than 50 years. Something about that day was strange, though. A few hours later, there was a second attack. A different bear hurt another woman.

 FAST FACT: About 20,000 grizzlies live in Canada. Alaska has about 30,000. Only about 1,800 live in the rest of the U.S. Most of those are in national parks.

CHAPTER 6
Small and Deadly

Big animals kill people. Some small ones do too. Venom is one of the tools they use. It packs a deadly punch.

Snakes

There are over 3,000 kinds of snakes in the world. A fifth of those use venom. Snakes use it to take down prey. They also use it in self-defense. People are not prey to these snakes. They just pose a danger. A person may surprise a snake. Someone may try to handle one. The snake wants to be left alone. It bites.

The inland Taipan lives in Australia. It has the strongest venom. One dose can kill 100 people. But the snake is shy. It would rather get away than fight. That keeps it from biting many.

FAST FACT: A gland near a snake's eye stores venom. A muscle pushes the liquid down the fangs.

34

35

CHAPTER 10
Killers That Don't Bite

Not all animals kill with bites. Some killers don't even have teeth. They are bugs.

Mosquitoes

One bug kills more than all others. It is the mosquito. They can carry disease. One is malaria. Yellow fever is another. The Zika virus is deadly too. These illnesses and others kill approximately 725,000 people each year. They make millions sick. Mosquitoes live all over the world. There are a few places without them. Most live in Africa and Asia.

Why are these bugs so deadly? One reason is how they eat. Females drink blood. They land on a person. Then they stab the skin with a tiny tube. It is like a needle. The tube gets blood. Germs get picked up too. Then the bug lands on the next person. The germs get passed on.

There is another reason for deaths. It is the number of these bugs. There are billions. They like warm and moist climates best. That describes many places.

FAST FACT: Mosquitoes are not all bad. They are food for many animals. Bats, birds, and frogs depend on them.

52

53

WH/TE L/GHTNING

BOOKS®

NONFICTION

9781680216387

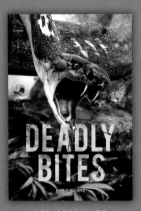

9781680216400

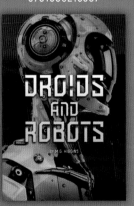

9781680216394

9781680216912

MORE TITLES COMING SOON

SDLBACK.COM/WHITE-LIGHTNING-BOOKS